Christian Discipleship and ME!

Narcissism's Impact Upon Our Understanding of Christian Discipleship

By
The Rev. Dr. Susan E. Lemly

Christian Discipleship and ME!

Lemly, Susan Eleanor, 1954 -

Published by
Total Support Group
Oceanside, California, 2001

1. Religion
2. Theology
3. Christian Ministry
4. Christian Discipleship
   I. Title

ISBN: 0-9710012-0-0

Total Support Group • Publishers

First Printing • 1k • r1
Printed in USA

Contents

Acknowledgements

This book would not have been possible were it not for the following people. These dear ones served as my hands and legs to function as scribes 'par excellence'. I love each of them and can never thank them enough for all they have done for me – Patty Walden, Marie Losh and Mary Jane Wissmann.

I deeply thank the Multiple Sclerosis Society for providing the funds for eight hours of Kelly Girl service each month. One of their especially fine workers was Carrie.

A great deal of gratitude and thanks goes to Ralph and Jeanne Brown who typed the manuscript and its revisions.

Thanks to Georgia Mattison–Glickel for her interest and assistance.

I also wish to thank the many caregivers who faithfully attended to my physical needs each day – Maxima Rodelo, Gerardo Olvera, Maria Zamora, Carlos Delgado, Gabby Barrera, Rosa Cortes, Molly Kaipio, Leslie Caldwell, and all the fine workers at Capistrano Beach Nursing Center.

A very special thanks to my dear friend and colleague, Bob Shuler, for writing the forward.

Dedication

To my precious parents:

Harry and Eleanor Lemly

"I love you and I miss you"

To my friend and typist:

Ralph E. Brown

"You were a kind, intelligent and elegant man"

Foreward

Dr. Lemly's book is a 'tour de force' on behalf of the Christian faith. Hers is a timely apology for the church. Like Jeremiah before her, this book has burned within Susan's stomach as a message that she had to get out. She wants society to know that Christian discipleship and narcissism cannot be reconciled. She seeks to clarify that indwelling of self is recklessly opposite to a dwelling within the Creator.

Susan has always been both a pastor and a theologian, and from these two vantage points, she has confronted chaos with clarity. Her illness over the years has ended her pastorates. Nevertheless, Susan remains an undaunted and vigorous theologian. She has done her homework in this, her first book, and done us all in the Church a significant favor. Readers, beware! This book will make you think, choose, change and confess anew God as Physician and Savior.

Bob Shuler, III
Senior Pastor at First United Methodist Church,
Riverside, California

❈ Chapter One ❉

"It is about time the piano realized it has not written the concerto!"[1]

"- All about Eve"

Aren't we all very much like the piano in the above quote? We assume that we have not only created our bodies but are in charge of life itself. An example of this thinking is defined in the theology of Paul Tillich. For Tillich, "ultimate concern" is faith in action and "ultimate reality" is our God. If our God is a false idol, it becomes unworthy of our "ultimate concern," and our devotion has been misplaced. An example of this falsehood is seen in people who have made their God "self." The achievement of a beautiful face and physique is how we express our devotion. The worst "Hell" these people may endure is having an unattractive face or a feeble body.

As much as we believe that we are monotheistic (believing in one God), the reality is that we are polytheistic. We believe in several gods. Among these gods are:

MOTHER NATURE: She is untamable and therefore inspires awe, surprise, and dread.

HERMAPHRODITUS[2]: The female/male god, empowered solely by our own desires. This god has an underused brain and extremely large genitalia which he/she displays with frequency and pride.

NO CONSEQUENCES: The god who enables us to harm others without accountability. An example of this god is found in Vincent Bugliosi's, *Outrage*.

> *"......and how could God, all-good and all-just, according to Christian theology, permit the person who murdered Ron and Nicole to go free, holding up a Bible in his hand at that?"[3]*

Bugliosi wryly comments that the guilt of Mr. Simpson's crime resides, not so much in Mr. Simpson's murderous brutality, as in the impotent and unjust Judeo-Christian God, contained in the Holy Bible that Simpson was waving triumphantly after his acquittal!

NO FORGIVENESS: In this god there is no mercy. Prayers to this god follow a pattern: pleas, superstitions, threats, and ultimately, indifference.

MAMMON (AKA MONEY): This god is worshipped with silent tones of reverence. Money itself bestows prestige and celebrity, two qualities highly valued in our modern culture.

Our final god is:

OURSELVES: The needs of each independent self are believed to be of ultimate importance and must be readily appeased.

Each of these gods thrives in a culture permeated with narcissism. Narcissism will result in the pursuit of superficial goals, i.e. the worshipful love of the body and the acquisition of prestigious things. These goals are far beneath the salvation Jesus has promised:

> *"Listen! I am standing at the door, knocking; if you hear my voice and open the door, I will come in to you and eat with you, and you with me."*
> *Revelation 3:20[4]*

Jesus' answer to deep-seated human moral weakness is love. First, love of God, and second, love of others as one's self.

The first is: *"Hear O Israel: the Lord our God, the Lord is one, you shall love the Lord your God with all your* heart, and with all your soul, and with all your mind, and with all your strength." The second is this: *"You shall love your neighbor as yourself."* There is no other commandment greater than these.

Mark 12:29-31

As the Apostle Paul describes the nature of Jesus Christ as one consumed with love for God and obedience to God's will, Jesus' life was filled with humility as He unselfishly sought to reveal God among us.

> *Do nothing from selfish ambition or conceit, but in humility regard others as better than yourselves. Let each of you look not to your own interests, but to the interests of others. Let the same mind be in you that was in Christ Jesus, who though he was in the form of God, did not regard equality with God as something to be exploited, but emptied himself taking the form of a slave, being born in human likeness. And being found in human form, he humbled himself and became obedient to the point of death - even death on a cross.*
>
> *Philippians 2:3-8*

It is difficult to imagine how we are capable of reconciling our current polytheism with Christian doctrine. This faith is what Dietrick Bonhoeffer would call "worldly Christianity." William E. Horden tells us about Bonhoeffer's thoughts on this subject.

The appeal to religion as inwardness corresponds to both the sacred-secular division and the god of the gaps. Man turns to his inner life, away from the world, to find the sacred realm. As man uses God to fill the gaps in his knowledge, so he turns to god as the "deus ex machina" to solve his personal problems when his own efforts run into a dead end. God becomes the cosmic bellhop to bring happiness to man and overcome his inward despair.[5]

As the Apostle Paul has written to the Colossians:

> *If with Christ you died to the elemental spirits of the universe, why do you live as if you still belonged to the world? Why do you submit to regulations...These have indeed an appearance of wisdom in promoting self imposed piety, humility, and severe treatment of the body, but they are of no value in checking self-indulgence.*
>
> *Colossians 3:20-21*

With what we have just read foremost in our minds, I offer the following chapters.

ENDNOTES - CHAPTER 1

1   Directed by Joseph L. Mankiecwicz and released by 20th Century Fox, <u>All About Eve</u>, 1950.

2   Copyright (c) 1996 Encyclopedia Britannica, Inc. All Rights Reserved.

> Hellenistic legend made Hermaphroditus a beautiful youth, the son of Hermes and Aphrodite. The nymph of the fountain of Salmacia in Caria became enamored of him and entreated the gods that she might be forever united with him. Her prayer answered, the result was the formation of a being half man, half woman. And so, in art we see a male/female minor divinity of sexual promiscuity and licentiousness.

3   Vincent Bugliosi, <u>Outrage, The Five Reasons Why O.J. Simpson Got Away With Murder</u> (New York, London: W. W. Norton and Company, 1996) Epilogue, p. 247

4   <u>Holy Bible</u> - New Revised Standard Version, published by Thomas Nelson for Cokesbury, Nashville and Burlingame. Text copyright 1990 by Graded Press (all further Biblical quotations are taken from this edition unless noted).

5   <u>A Layman's Guide to Protestant Theology</u>, William E. Horden. McMillan Publishing Co. Inc. New York, Collier McMillian Publishers, London, Eighth Printing 1974, p.220

❈{ Chapter Two }❊

NARCISSISM DEFINED

There is a great deal of confusion surrounding the term "narcissism": what phenomenon it describes and how it is to be used. Grace Stuart quotes Henry H. Hart as stating that:

> *When in psychoanalytic literature such varied phenomena as a state of sleep, a baby sucking its thumb, a girl primping before a mirror, and a scientist exulting in the Nobel Prize are all referred to as "narcissistic" a more precise definition of the term seems indicated.*[2]

Heinz Kohut's definition of narcissism as the "libidinal investment of the self" does not bring a conclusion to the controversy between scholars over the use of the term.[3] But first, I will present the myth of Narcissus.

THE MYTH

The original version of the myth is found in Book III of METAMORPHOSIS by Ovid. By Ovid's account, when Narcissus was born, his mother, Leiriope, went to Tiresias, the seer, to inquire about the child's future. Tiresias told her, "Narcissus will live to be a ripe old age, provided he never knows himself."

Narcissus grew to be a very beautiful young man. Many fell in love with him, but he scorned them all. One nymph, angered at the cruel rejection of the love offered, prayed that Narcissus would one day fall in love and have his love rejected. Nemisis, hearing the prayer, responded by leading Narcissus to a pool of water to drink. At this pool Narcissus saw his own reflection and fell in love, thinking that the reflection he saw was the face of another person.

His attempt to embrace the reflection was futile, for when he reached toward it, he disturbed the water and the image fled. When the water stilled, the image reappeared and seemed to welcome him, only to flee once more at his touch. His fascination with the image grew as he sat by the pool and repeated the tragic cycle.

Finally, Narcissus, grieving over the repeated separation, implored the image to remain with him so that he could gaze upon it, even if he could not embrace it. At last, Narcissus understood his tragedy. "I burn with love of my own self." His love could not be reciprocated for there was no <u>other</u> to return it. He died of self-consuming love.[4]

Here are portions of Edith Hamilton's recounting of the myth of Narcissus:

> *Narcissus' beauty was so great, all the girls who saw him longed to be his, but he would have none of them. So Narcissus went on his cruel way, a scorner of love. But at last one of those he wounded prayed a prayer and it was answered by the gods: "May he who loves not others love himself." The great goddess Nemesis, which means righteous anger, undertook to bring this about. As Narcissus bent over a clear pool for a drink and saw there his own reflection, on the moment he fell in love with it. "Now I know," he cried, "what others have suffered from me, for I burn with love of my own self - and yet how can I reach that loveliness I see mirrored in the water? I cannot leave it. Only death can set me free." And so it happened. He pined away, leaning perpetually over the pool, fixed in one long gaze.[5]*

The picture of Narcissus given in the myth speaks of a deeply disturbing phenomenon — the rejection of the self. Although Narcissus pleads with the reflection not to reject him, it repeatedly does as he reaches to embrace it. Shirley Sugarman suggests that this implies self-rejection, "a sense of worthlessness and of rage turned inward."[6] Narcissus' despair is heightened by the rejection of the only "other" present in his life. The terror and dread created by this knowledge led to his death. As Sugarman states, "Narcissus reveals a powerful illustration of what sin involves—a profound sense of worthlessness and rejection resulting in self-destruction."[7] His self-love was simply a mask for an unbearable sense of lovelessness, estrangement, and separation.

One thing is made very clear in the myth: narcissism is not a benign malady. Narcissus died of his condition. Grace Stuart recognizes the self-destructive emphasis of the myth and states that "narcissism is a deplorable state which must be outgrown, both by the individual and by humanity."[8] As the Apostle Paul wrote to the Corinthians:

> *When I was a child, I spoke like a child, I thought like a child, I reasoned like a child; when I became an adult, I put an end to childish ways.*
> *I Cor. 13:11*

THE TERM

The myth of Narcissus has captivated the imagination of writers for centuries. In 1850 Herman Melville wrote:

> *And deeper the meaning of that story of Narcissus, who because he could not grasp*

the tormenting, mild image he saw in the fountain, plunged into it and was drowned. But that same image, we ourselves see in all rivers and oceans. It is the image of the ungraspable phantom of life, and this is the key to it all.[9]

The words "narcissism" and "narcissistic" do not appear until the writings of Remy de Gourmont and Valera respectively. De Gourmont wrote:

...what we see clearly and deliciously as in a mirror is ourselves, remoulded and made more beautiful by love. It follows that when we think we love another being, it is ourselves that we love, and as that other one is subject to the same illusion with regard to us, the two lovers are under the impression that they are giving themselves and taking each other, whereas they are merely taking themselves and giving themselves to their own egoism...From the purely idealistic point of view narcissism would be the supreme formula of love...[10]

For this insight, he may have relied upon some psychological reading. But, it is doubtful that he relied upon Freud, for Freud asserted that narcissism has to do with what he called object-love, or the choice of another to love which resembles the self. Of this notion de Gourmont appears skeptical for he believes that the narcissist does not transcend the self even to this degree.[11]

Valera, in 1887, published a notable volume of short stories which first used the term "narcissistic." In one of her stories, the heroine, after her bath, says: "I behave like a narcissist: I place my lips on the cold surface of my mirror, and I kiss my own image."[12]

This quotation is an example of the narcissist being one who sexually falls in love with oneself. This meaning influenced the psychological definition of the term in that it define narcissism as "falling in love with the mirror-image."[13]

The thrust of this early definition can be seen in Havelock Ellis's 1898 description of narcissism as auto-eroticism. By narcissism, Ellis means the narcissist-like tendency (a phrase he coined) involves the absorption of sexual emotions in self-admiration. Näcke summarized Ellis' article and coined the term "Narcismus" which later became the term "narcissism".

Freud, in 1910 took the term from Näcke and used it to describe what he called "sexual inversion". He used the term "narcissism" in a casual sense at first, but in 1914 he began to see the more serious implications of it. In his article he examined what he called "primary narcissism", the first stage of early life. He writes: "We form a conception of an original libidinal cathexis of the ego,"[14] evidencing his suspicion that the self could love itself in much the same way it could love an object. Stuart states that by his statement he appears to consider narcissism normal; but his position is apparently confused by his reference to autoeroticism as being a primordial instinct. Narcissism must then be an element added to autoeroticism, as Stuart suggests in her analysis of his work.[15]

J. C. Flugel follows this conclusion by Freud and suggests that two primordial stages exist. The earliest libidinal stage involves autoeroticism and, as a second stage, narcissism. He illustrates these stages by this example "the eating of sweets may be autoerotic, while to refrain from eating sweets...in order not to become overweight would be narcissistic: one would...give oneself pleasure in the comeliness of one's body and its image rather than give pleasure to one's body."[16]

Edward Glover is another psychologist willing to state that narcissism "is a perfectly normal stage of development" and, along with Marjorie Brierly and Melanie Klien, attributes many positive effects to it as well. But as Stuart points out, even among these writers in "the next moment, the next page, the next chapter, narcissism is pathological, unhealthy, regressive, malign, it veritably sprouts disorder, it is neurotic, psychotic, psychosomatic."[17] Various psychological writers attempt to lessen this contradiction through the use of qualifying adjectives, either pathological or benevolent. These adjectives do not quell the presence of contradictory uses of this term, but merely establish further confusion.

The question arises after examining these writers and psychoanalysts: is narcissism genuine self-love or not? Conflicting answers exist among these people. De Gourmont, Valera, and Ellis assert that narcissism is an indication of the sexual love of the self. Freud and Flugel state that narcissism can have both positive and negative aspects - both healthy and neurotic manifestations. Glover, Brierly, and Klien each affirm the positive effect of narcissism on the personality, while Stuart posits that narcissism has a purely negative effect upon the self. As Stuart claims: "When the picture is traced in more careful detail, when we see there a person who both kills and dies, the term seems more properly to apply to one of the gravest of mental ills."[18]

In the next chapter we will discuss the relationship between narcissism and self-love. Heinz Kohut, Otto Kernberg and Béla Grunberger are psychoanalysts who believe that narcissism can assume a positive form and that this form may readily be called healthy self-love. But Stuart disagrees with this position and states that the term "narcissism" must be applied to a condition of self-hatred and isolation. For her, narcissism can only have self-destructive consequences.

The possibility of healthy narcissism does not exist.

We will place Martin Luther's and Jean Calvin's discussion of self-knowledge alongside the arguments of these four writers in order to determine whether narcissism conflicts with or upholds healthy self-love. Luther and Calvin speak of self-love as an aspect of self-knowledge as essential to one's relationship with God. Their perspectives will begin to show how narcissism relates to Christianity.

ENDNOTES - CHAPTER TWO

1   Cartoon: "Crock" by Bill Rechin and Don Wilder, 1992; North American Syndicate, Inc. World rights reserved.

2   Grace Stuart, NARCISSUS (London, Allen and Unwin, 1956) p. 22.

3   Heinz Kohut, THE SEARCH FOR THE SELF (New York: International Press, 1978), p. 427.

4   Ovid, METAMORPHOSIS, Book III, from Robert Graves, THE GREEK MYTHS, quoted by Shirley Sugarman, SIN AND MADNESS, (Philadelphia: Westminster Press, 1979), p. 19f.f.

5   MYTHOLOGY, Edith Hamilton (Little, Brown and Company, Boston,Massachusetts, 1942), pp. 113-115.

6   Sugarman, Shirley, SIN AND MADNESS: STUDIES IN NARCISSISM, (Philadelphia, Westminster Press, 1979), p. 22.

7   Ibid., p. 22.

8   Stuart, p. 30. Walter Zimmerli notes how separation, isolation, is not only bad, but in fact constitutes sin in the Old Testament:

> *"..... sin shows in horrible distortion how man was created for life with others, and how even here it is not good for him to be alone."*
> *Gen. 2:18*

       Walter Zimmerli, OLD TESTAMENT THEOLOGY IN OUTLINE (Atlanta: John Knox Press, 1978), p. 169.

9   Ibid, p. 24

10   Ibid

11   Ibid

12   Ibid, p. 25

13   Ibid

1 4   Sigmund Freud, COLLECTED PAPERS, IV, New York:B a s i c
        Books, 1959, p. 45, 48

1 5   Stuart, pp 25, 26

1 6   Ibid., p. 25. J. C. Flugel writes about Freud on narcissism in,
        Man, Morals and Society (New York: International and
        University Press, 1945), pp. 34-35. Flugel's discussion of
        Freud's position that narcissism involves objective love
        directed toward the self agrees with Stuart's treatment of
        Freud.

1 7   Ibid, p. 28

1 8   Ibid, p. 30

❖ Chapter Three ❖

"Did we in our own strength confide,
Our striving would be losing,
Were not the right man on our side,
The man of God's own choosing.
Dost ask who that may be?
Christ Jesus, it is he;
Lord Sabaoth, his name,
From age to age the same,

and he must win the battle."

A MIGHTY FORTRESS IS OUR GOD

Martin Luther

NARCISSISM AND SELF-LOVE

In the last chapter we related the myth of Narcissus and wrote how there is confusion surrounding the use of the term "narcissism." Much of the controversy surrounding the use of the term narcissism stems from concern over whether it is a proper term to use for both positive and negative self-love. We mentioned that the myth, ending in tragedy and death, does not lend itself well to a term which is supposed to describe healthy self-love. These issues are the focus of this chapter.

A review of several descriptions of narcissism were given in Chapter Two. De Gourmont asserted that narcissism involves romantic love of the self. Valera characterized narcissism as love for one's mirror image. Ellis felt that narcissism involves autoeroticism or the investment of one's sexual emotions in the self. Freud at first asserted that narcissism involves sexual inversion but later held that it is a normal stage of early life. Flugel divided narcissism into two stages: the first being autoeroticism (the earliest libidinal stage) and the second being narcissism proper. De Gourmont and Valera offer literary descriptions while Ellis, Freud, and Flugel make early attempts at psychoanalytic definitions. Each of these writers offer important insights into the meaning of the term narcissism, but confusion over its use remains. Can narcissism effectively define healthy self-love or not?

In order to answer this question I will examine Heinz Kohut, Otto Kernberg, and Béla Grunberger, three psychoanalytic writers who have recently dealt with the characteristics of narcissism. Stuart contributes to the understanding of narcissism from the perspective of one who has taught in the area of journalism and holds a Bachelor of Literature degree based upon a thesis in the area of psychology. We will also examine Martin Luther and John Calvin on the importance of self-knowledge to faith and knowledge of God.

Chapter Three

THE SELF IN PSYCHOANALYTIC THEORY

Kohut, Kernberg, and Grunberger have done a great deal of study in the area of narcissism. Their work is widely respected in psychoanalytic circles. Kohut is the most popular of the three and has been featured in the magazine TIME. In the magazine article his basic position in the area of narcissism is noted to include both negative and positive elements. Kohut asserts that emotional deprivation leads to the development of negative narcissism, while positive narcissism enables one to love and care for the self.

Kernberg affirms that narcissism includes both positive and negative elements as does Kohut. Kernberg characterizes narcissism, on the positive side, as involving the development of "self-esteem" and "self-regard." Negative narcissism involves self-disintegration and loss of the self. Positive narcissism assists in the development of an integrated self and ultimately self-love.

Grunberger writes that the term narcissism is difficult to define, but he affirms with Kohut and Kernberg that it can have either positive or negative manifestations. He notes that narcissism is an energizing factor which assists in the survival of a person.

Each of these psychoanalysts refers to Freud's article <u>On Narcissism: An Introduction.</u> Freud's article provided a basis from which these psychoanalysts departed in their study of narcissism: its characteristics and treatment. Kohut, Kernberg, and Grunberger use Freud as a basis for asserting that a healthy form of narcissism exists. Freud makes this position clear with the statement that:

Narcissism ...(is) not... a perversion, but the libidinal complement to the egoism of the instinct of self-preservation, a measure of which may justifiably be attributed to every living creature.[1]

He makes this statement from the perspective that narcissism may well be a part of the "regular sexual development of human beings."[2]

Freud divided the concept of narcissism into two categories: primary and normal narcissism. These terms have readily been adopted by colleagues in the field of psychoanalysis. He also isolated two characteristics of narcissism pointed out by others later, namely, megalomania and the withdrawal of interest in the outside world, i.e., people and things.

The following psychoanalysis began with Freud's categories of primary and normal narcissism. The way in which they develop these categories is a mark of each one's own research and scholarship.

Heinz Kohut

Heinz Kohut provided the definition of narcissism used in the first and second chapter, namely, narcissism as the "libidinal investment of the self."[3] As noted in Chapter Two, this definition is not held by all psychoanalysts in the field of narcissism, but it serves as an important function for the comprehension of Kohut's work.

Kohut asserts that narcissism is a healthy element of human development. He feels that negative opinions of narcissism come from a comparison between narcissism and object love, with narcissism being labeled as "the more primitive and the less adaptive of the two forms of libido distribution."[4] He immediately refutes this opinion as not based upon an objective assessment of narcissism, either as a developmental stage or as a characteristic possessing valuable adaptive potential. Rather, this opinion stems from "the improper intrusion of the altruistic value system of Western civilization."[5] He explains that negative judgments upon narcissism "exert a narrowing effect on clinical practice...(and) tend to lead to a wish from the side of the therapist to replace the patient's narcissistic position with object love..."[6] Negative assessments of narcissism are also partially due to the fact that therapists predominantly have contact with narcissistic persons in a state of disturbance ("narcissistic injury"), rather than the person manifesting "silent states of narcissism in equilibrium..."[7] Because of the therapists' contact with the negative side of narcissism he feels that the healthy side of narcissism has been ignored by psychoanalysts.

Kohut relies heavily upon the work of Freud for his understanding of narcissism but differs with Freud over what is the central struggle of human development. Freud asserts that it is the Oedipal struggle, or the child's desire for the parent of the opposite sex, and the rage of the child because this is ultimately thwarted by the power of the parent of the same sex. Kohut believes that it is the narcissistic struggle which involves the development of a healthy self-love.

Kohut adopts Freud's term, "primary narcissism," and defines it as the stage in infant life wherein the child does not differentiate between himself or herself and the mother. Ultimately the child will become disappointed in the mother's ministrations because of her imperfection, and a trauma for the baby will ensue. This stage involves the development of what Freud calls the "purified pleasure ego" or the stage "in which everything pleasant, good, and perfect is regarded as part of a rudimentary self, while everything unpleasant, bad, and imperfect is regarded as 'outside'."[8]

Kohut regards the "purified pleasure ego" as a presage or early developmental element in what he refers to as the "narcissistic self." The narcissistic self is a structure within the personality which resembles the ego ideal in that it contains the ambitions and ideals of the self. It is both a maturational and developmental achievement and is the portion of the personality readily damaged by emotional deprivation or repression. The narcissistic self is one pole Kohut uses to describe differentiated primary narcissism. The other is the "idealized parent imago," or the internally developed image of the perfect parent that protects the self from frustration.

For Kohut, primary narcissism lingers within a person in these two differentiated forms. The idealized parent imago exists as an aspect of narcissism in that it is still undifferentiated as part of the infant self that projects all power, perfection, and goodness upon the parent. This notion changes through maturation and is influenced by a child's cognitive development and "environmental factors that affect the choice of internalization and their intensity."[9]

A premature loss of the parent through death, absence, or withdrawal of affection through mental or physical illness causes internalization in the child. Internalization involves projecting the idealized parent upon the self and causes the formation of an idealized superego. This process can lead at a later time to a vacillation between a person's desire to attach oneself to omnipotent powers outside of the self and develop a grandiose notion of the self and its powers.[10] This response may be later transformed into a pathological state.

The developments of the narcissistic self is characterized by Kohut as both a "maturationally predetermined step and as a developmental achievement..."[11] A premature interruption of this process leads to later vulnerability from problems caused by the unmodified grandiose fantasy. In other words, a healthy sense of the limitations of the self is not developed or integrated into the personality structure.

Kohut isolates two characteristics of narcissism:

exhibitionism and the grandiose fantasy. Exhibitionism is regarded by him to be the primary narcissistic drive. Narcissistic exhibitionism emphasizes the self as performer rather than the other as observer. The observer has importance only as a participant in the pleasure of the narcissist.

Kohut states that this exhibitionist tendency eventually becomes subordinated to an individual's goal-directed activities. This is accomplished through gradually frustrating exhibitionistic tendencies in an atmosphere of love and support. Without this atmosphere the narcissist is open to developing a wide range of emotional disturbances, varying from hypochondria to simple embarrassment.

While exhibitionism may be considered the predominate drive of the narcissist, the grandiose fantasy is the idealized content of the self. Whether this characteristic contributes to a person's health and success or disease and downfall has much to do with whether or not it has been successfully integrated into the ego. This transference is accomplished through the individual's early internalization of the attitude that he or she is either a conqueror or a failure. A positive internalization of this characteristic can contribute to a person's later success. Freud used this assertion to point out the adaptive value of narcissism.

Kohut summarizes the effect of exhibitionism and the grandiose fantasy upon the developing self by stating:

> *narcissistic-exhibitionistic tensions remain undischarged, become dammed up,....the emotion of disappointment that the ego experiences always contains an admixture of shame. And if the grandiosity of the narcissistic self has been insufficiently modified because traumatic onslaughts on*

> *the child's self-esteem have driven the*
> *grandiose fantasies into repression, then the*
> *adult ego will tend to vacillate between an*
> *irrational overestimation of the self and*
> *feeling of inferiority, and will react with*
> *narcissistic mortification. . .to the*
> *thwarting of its ambitions.*[12]

The two narcissistic qualities isolated by Kohut manifest themselves through the healthy enjoyment of one's activities and successes, while having an adaptively appropriate awareness of disappointment mixed with anger and shame at one's failure. Similarly the grandiose fantasy, shaped by the internalization of reality, becomes the ego ideal and is capable of lending to the self an important and healthy sense of pursuing an objective or goal as well as the adaptive sensation of disappointment if unable to attain it. [13]

Otto Kernberg

Otto Kernberg agrees with Kohut that narcissism is a normal quality of development that can be healthy or pathological, depending upon the social environment of the developing child. Kernberg accepts the definition used by Kohut, the "libidinal investment of the self," as the definition of healthy narcissism.

Healthy narcissism is characterized by him as involving a self that has successfully integrated both good and bad self-images creating a realistic self-concept. The integrated self not only contains normal "self-feeling" or personal experience of integration, but it also contains "self-esteem" or "self-regard" which depends upon the investment of libidinal energy in the self and leads to the coordination of the self and other "intrapsychic structures." These intrapsychic structures include the ego, the superego, and the id. The absence of an integrated self is "characterized by chronic feelings of unreality, puzzlement, emptiness, or general disturbances in the 'self-feeling' as well as. . .a marked incapacity to perceive oneself realistically as a total human being."[14] In other words, the self is fragmented into several seemingly unrelated traits. This self disintegration is characterized by a loss of the self and a feeling of emptiness.

Kernberg states that normal narcissism is influenced by several intrapsychic structures as well as external factors. He divides these intrapsychic structures into five categories:

1. The Ideal Self and Ego Goals
2. Object Representations
3. Superego Factors
4. Instinctual and Organic Factors
5. External Factors[15]

In the first category, the ideal self and ego goals, Kernberg states that the actual self is measured against three subcategories of the ego: unconscious, preconscious and conscious ego goals. Self-esteem is regulated and ultimately achieved by such self-criticism. The process enables one to cope with the tension between the real and ideal self.[16]

Object representations is the second category and describes the process of relating the "world of inner objects" to the integrated self. This process is another function of the ego involving the regulation of self-esteem. Through this process one is able to cope with life crisis or object loss by reactivating the memory of an internalized good experience from one's past. Kernberg states that the memory of a good object relation or relationship enables one to reinforce one's self-image through recalling that one is indeed loved.[17]

In the third category, superego factors, Kernberg writes about the two major structures of the superego which regulate self-esteem. The first of these is made up of several levels which carry out the critical evaluation of the ego upon the demands of the superego. Kernberg notes Edith Jacobson at this point by stating that her analysis of these levels of the superego is that these regulate the self through moods or realistic self-criticism. The second structure of the superego, involving self-esteem regulation once again, is the ego ideal. The ego ideal is formed through the integration of ideal object-images and ideal self-images developed in infancy and early childhood. It is capable in increasing self-esteem when one lives up to the demands and expectations it projects. A person who is over-dependent upon others for love and admiration has not successfully integrated this superego structure into the personality.

The fourth of these categories, instinctual and organic factors, is related to the id.[18] This category has a great deal to do with one's physical health and appearance. The presence of illness in the body significantly influences the equilibrium of this system and upsets the libidinal investment of the self.

The fifth and final category, external factors, deals with what Kernberg calls "reality factors influencing the normal regulation of self-esteem."[19] These are: "1) libidinal gratifications stemming from external objects; 2) gratification of ego goals and aspirations in social effectiveness or success; and 3) gratification of intellectual or cultural aspirations realized in the environment."[20] These subcategories reflect the demands of the superego as well as various elements of reality. They are important in terms of regulating self-esteem in the presence of cultural, ethical, and esthetics value demands.

Each of these five categories, in Kernberg's estimation, contributes to healthy narcissism and ultimately to the healthy self. He summarizes their value by stating that where "there is an increase of libidinal investment of the self with love or gratification from external objects, success in reality, increase of harmony between the self and superego structures, reconfirmation of love from internal objects....direct instinctual gratification and physical health" one is most likely to see the presence of healthy narcissism.[21]

Kernberg divides pathological narcissism into three groups, the third group demonstrating the most severe disturbance. The first group examines the presence of narcissistic tendencies and their function in protecting and maintaining self-esteem. The more rigidly these pathological tendencies adhere, the more likely one is to find the presence of intrapsychic disturbance.

The second group isolated by Kernberg in the area of pathological narcissism is the group exhibiting narcissistic fixation. This group also displays "defenses linked with all kinds of genital or pre-genital conflicts; the infantile-narcissistic aspects of many hysterical and obsessive tendencies are typical examples".[22]

The third category is pathological narcissism proper. This category manifests "a specific character constellation which reflects a particular pathology of internalized object relationships, and particular distortions of ego and superego structures."[23] The term "narcissism" is used in the narrow sense when describing this category and in the broad sense when describing the first two categories. This third category may be considered the most seriously disturbed.

Kernberg proposes that these categories of pathological narcissism share several tendencies. These tendencies include a feeling of emptiness and futility, a persistent sense of restlessness and boredom, and an inability to deal with and overcome normal loneliness. For the narcissist the normal relationship "between the self the internal world of objects.... is threatened."[24] The world of the narcissist is filled with uncertainty and loneliness because of his or her grandiosity and inability to perceive another as separate from the self; a narcissist is unable to have genuine empathy toward humanity. The social life they participate in is able to give them a sense of meaningfulness as well as fulfill their need for admiration, but this satisfaction is only temporary. When a sense of gratification has passed, emptiness, restlessness and boredom return. As Kernberg states, the world of the narcissist is a "prison from which only new excitement, admiration, or experiences implying control, triumph or incorporation of supplies are an escape."[25]

Béla Grunberger

Béla Grunberger also approaches the topic of narcissism through the work of Freud. This perspective flavors his work and influences his choice of terminology. Grunberger takes into account the way in which the term is presently understood by analysts. He, with Kohut and Kernberg, believes that narcissism is an attribute which can have either healthy or pathological manifestations. In spite of the obvious contradictions between writers, Grunberger finds enough material to present a consistent picture of narcissism and its tendencies.[26]

Much of his work is an echo of Kohut and Kernberg, possibly because they all begin with Freud's work on narcissism. Grunberger sees in the narcissist an effort to recover the lost omnipotence of infancy through identification with the parent imago. Inevitably instinctual frustrations will cancel out the ability of the child to find relief through hallucinatory gratification and the narcissist will cease to see others as others, thus decreasing his or her frustration. The process just described leads to the loss of self, emptiness, and grandiosity described by Kohut and Kernberg. This fits well with Freud's description of narcissism as "the victorious assertion of the ego's invulnerability."[27]

Grunberger asserts that narcissism is present from birth and remains with us throughout life. He describes it as an energizing factor which has the qualities of an instinct; yet narcissism transcends instinctual manifestations. Narcissism can be "discerned beneath them, as if it were their underlying motivation and prime cause."[28]

Grunberger differs with Freud, Kohut, and Kernberg in that he does not see narcissism as part of the ego ideal. Rather, Grunberger posits that narcissism is an autonomous factor and should be viewed from this perspective. He defines narcissism as a "psychic agency along with the id, the ego, and the superego."[29] He believes that by doing this, "conferring on narcissism the rank of agency or motive force"[30], confusion concerning its definition will decrease.

From the work of these three people one receives the understanding that narcissism is a normal feature in human development. Kohut, Kernberg, and Grunberger each affirms that narcissism can be either a healthy or pathological quality, depending upon the infant's early experience with the mother.

Grace Stuart

Stuart does not negate self-love as a necessary and vital element in psychic health, but she does not see in narcissism the potential for developing genuine self-love. As mentioned in chapter two, the legend of Narcissus ends in tragedy and death. Any term which harkens back to this myth must incorporate this fact. The attempt of Kohut, Kernberg, and Grunberger to speak of healthy narcissism is a false use of the original myth. As Stuart states "love of self cannot be thought of as destroying,......and anything which does destroy is not love."[31]

Stuart characterizes the narcissist as one who maintains infantile traits throughout life. He or she is a subject without an object, a self without an other. All of his or her love-objects are solely within the self and he or she identifies with them alone. He or she is extremely isolated and withdrawn, inaccessible to other's interest and affection. The ability to love is nonexistent for "Loving...demands the greatest possible adaptation to the external world and at the same time makes the greatest breach in primary narcissism, which cannot bear that anything should exist outside itself..."[32]

Stuart states that the narcissist is a person without a self. Her term for this is the "not-self." The body continues to grow and develop while the interior self remains infantile, causing the development of a "kind of monstrosity."[33]

Stuart states that selfishness is indeed a characteristic of the narcissist, but it is a secondary characteristic. Immaturity is the primary characteristic in the narcissist from which selfishness becomes the expression. It is a characteristic of the not-self.

In Narcissus we see a figure who has been destroyed through his isolation. He rejected the love of others in favor of loving an image which was incapable of returning his love. The knowledge that the isolated self is the destructive self is a part of human consciousness from the earliest times. In Genesis 2:18a the writer has God say, "It is not good that the man should be alone..." Isolation and separation is not good. It leads to the destruction of that which is created good by God, namely, a healthy self in communion with others.

Martin Luther and Jean Calvin discuss self-love from a theological and anthropological perspective and state that self-love, as well as love of God, are bound up in self-knowledge. We will now explore self-knowledge in Luther and Calvin.

THE SELF IN LUTHER AND CALVIN

The healthy self in Luther and Calvin is the self turned toward God in obedience, adoration, and trust. Self-knowledge is a vital element of one's faith in and devotion to God. This is not the kind of self-knowledge Tiresias warned Narcissus' mother about. It is not self-knowledge from the perspective of an unchangeable fate, rather self-knowledge for Luther and Calvin is awareness of oneself as a child of God, sinful yet loved and valued by God. In the myth of Narcissus the realization of his condition is the final step which leads to his death. He perceives his condition from the point of futility, never thinking that the opportunity to turn from the river toward those who love him is possible. Narcissus remains with his own reflection until he dies.

This is the great peril of modern humans as well. Guiding people to the place in which they realize that they can turn from the river toward a genuine love is the challenge of ministers of Jesus Christ today. André Gide, in Le Traité du Narcisse, believes that Narcissus was man himself, gazing into the river of time. If he would turn back from the river, he might see other things to love, but he does not turn. This is the task of all who follow Jesus Christ, enabling people to turn away from the river of self-absorption and death toward the love of God, self, and others, and abundant life in Christ.

Luther writes in his commentary on Romans about human nature being bound "to original sin,....so curved in upon itself at its deepest levels that it not only bends the best gifts of God toward itself in order to enjoy them..., nay, rather, 'uses' God in order to obtain them...(Our perverted nature) ...seeks everything, including God, only for itself."[34] This is the same condition Shirley Guthrie decries in mentioning that people use God as a "great heavenly candy machine"[35] with the candy being self-fulfillment. For fundamentalists the candy takes the form of personal salvation; for the charismatic it is personal joy, peace and religious ecstasy; for the liberals it is the victory of whatever cause or movement with which they identify; and for "white middle-class Americans of all theological stripes....it is political superiority, economic security, physical comfort and, above all, happiness."[36] The emphasis of this last classification was abundantly evident in the 1980 election and was present among all classes in American culture, not just the middle-class. God has been equated with these goals in American society, by all classes, to the point where people no longer differentiate between these implied values and the will of God.

Luther continues to write, "Thus man learns to love and worship God unconditionally, i.e., to worship him not for the sake of grace and its gifts but solely for his own sake."[37] A relationship with God requires that we turn away from the river of self-absorption as it manifests itself in both perceived personal needs and larger cultural values.

Self-knowledge, in the sense that Luther describes, involves the softening of the human heart. Luther writes how God has hardened the hearts of humans, as God did to Satan and the Pharaoh of Egypt, because of our ungodliness. Humans do not seek the will of God, but rather his or her "own riches, and glory, and works, and sovereignty in everything..."[38] A person can no more "restrain his fury than he can stop his self-seeking, he can no more stop his self-seeking than he can stop his existing - - for he is still a creature of God, though a spoiled one."[39]

Luther maintains that true self-knowledge and

knowledge of God are bound together, and one must know oneself in combination with knowledge and adoration of God in order to experience grace. Herein lies a person's freedom: complete knowledge of the self and one's distortion along with the knowledge that God loves and desires a person's turning and repentance. Luther's fourth thesis, in the famous Ninety-five Theses, is that "As long as hatred of self abides... the penalty of sin abides."[40] We must flee from self-hatred and all its trappings as we would sin itself.[41]

Narcissism leads to the death of a person and so does sin. Transformations, or repentance, must take place or the person will die in hopelessness, psychic pain, and isolation.

Calvin writes about the importance of self-knowledge even more explicitly than Luther. He states quite emphatically in his Institutes that "Without knowledge of self there is no knowledge of God."[42] He writes that all time and sound wisdom we possess "consists of two parts: the knowledge of God and of ourselves."[43] We must contemplate "our own ignorance, vanity, poverty, infirmity, ... depravity and corruption" before we can discover that God alone possesses the "true light of wisdom, sound virtue, full abundance of every good, and purity of righteousness..."[44] Contemplating our own unhappiness and distortion permits us to learn humility and "attain at least some knowledge of God."[45] So long as we remain ignorant of our poverty, ignorance and misery, true knowledge of God will elude us. The tragedy of the myth of Narcissus lies in the fact that even in self-knowledge, the knowledge of his misery, Narcissus does not perceive the opportunity to turn away from this misery toward life. Death was the only option he perceived. As the Apostle Paul writes, ". . . how are men to call upon him in whom they have not believed? And how are they to believe in him of whom they have never heard? And how are they to hear without a preacher?..." (Rom. 10:14a RSV). All christians who have received and accepted the call of Jesus Christ can make Him known to every narcissist in our society.

Calvin also states that without knowledge of God there can be no self-knowledge. He maintains that a human:

> ...never achieves a clear knowledge of himself unless he has first looked upon God's face. . . For we always seem to ourselves righteous and upright and wise and holy. This pride is innate in all of us, unless by clear proofs we stand convinced of our own unrighteousness, foulness, folly, and impurity.[46]

Genuine self-knowledge is therefore contingent upon knowledge of the mystery and majesty of God. Humans are able to deceive themselves about their true nature until they compare themselves with God, or, as Calvin writes, ". . .so long as we confine our minds within the limits of human corruption."[47] If humans continue to look upon themselves as the only point of reality, genuine self-knowledge will continue to elude them. Narcissus' perception of his isolation and misery remained the only perception available to him because of his unwillingness to turn away; knowledge of God and self is mutually connected. Knowledge of God must precede genuine knowledge of the self.

Luther and Calvin each affirm the importance of self-knowledge in relation to knowledge of God. The denial of the self of which Jesus spoke, does not require self-ignorance. Denial of the self involves transcendence of the self wherein the human perceives his or her needs in relation to the majesty, love, and justice of God. According to Tillich, in God's love and one's belief in Jesus as the Christ, we transcend all, even finitude and the negative self absorption that precedes it.

Self-knowledge in Luther and Calvin alike is vital for knowledge of God. They assert that genuine self-knowledge is important and must take place through one's comparison with God. The importance of comparing oneself with God is not mentioned by the psychoanalysts, and is distorted by the religious narcissists, who form an image of God in respect to their needs. These problems will be explored in the next chapter when I will examine how Tillich's thought compares on the condition of sin and the negative characteristics of narcissism. The similarities contain important implications for the transformation of narcissism and how the church needs to address the modern world.

ENDNOTES - CHAPTER THREE

1   Sigmund Freud, <u>COLLECTED PAPERS</u>, IV, (New York: Basic Books, 1959), p. 31.

2   Ibid., p. 30.

3   Heinz Kohut, <u>The Search For the Self</u> (New York: International Press, 1978), p. 427.

4   Heinz Kohut, <u>The Analysis of the Self</u> (New York:International Press, 1971), p. 427.

5   Ibid.

6   Ibid.

7   Ibid., p. 428.

8   Ibid., p. 430.

9   Ibid., p. 432. Kohut states that "the difference between the idealized parent imago and the narcissistic self is that the idealized parent is looked up to and admired while the narcissistic self wants to be looked at and admired." pp. 438-439.

10   Kohut, <u>The Analysis</u>..., p. 433.

11   Ibid., p. 438.

12   Ibid., p. 440.

13   Ibid.

14   Otto Kernberg, <u>Borderline Conditions and Pathological Narcissism</u> (New York: Jason Aronaon, 1975), p. 316.

15   Ibid., p. 318 f.f.

16   Ibid., p. 318.

17   Ibid., p. 320.

18   "Id - the primitive, instinctual, childish, unconscious portion of the personality that obeys the pleasure principle." James V. McConnel, <u>Understanding Human Behavior</u> (New York: Holt, Rinehard and Winston, 1974), p. 615.

19   Kernberg, p. 320.

20   Ibid.

21   Ibid.

22.   Ibid.

23   Ibid., p. 115

24   Ibid.

25   Ibid., p. 213.

26   Béla Grunberger, <u>Narcissism</u> (New York: International University Press, 1971) p. 103.

27   Ibid., p. 104.

28   Ibid., p. 106.

29   Ibid., p. 108.

30   Ibid.

31   Grace Stuart, <u>Narcissus</u> (London: Allen and Unwin, 1956), p. 125·

32   Ibid., p. 154.

33   Ibid., p. 155.

34   Martin Luther, <u>Lectures on Romans</u> (Philadelphia: Westminster Press, 1961) p. 159.

35   Shirley C. Guthrie, Jr., "The Narcissism of American Piety: The Disease and the Cure," <u>Journal of Pastoral Care</u>, XXXI (December 1977), p. 160.

36   Ibid.

37   Luther, p. 160.

38   Martin Luther, <u>Selections from His Writings</u> (Garden City: Doubleday, 1961), p. 192.

39   Ibid., p. 194.

40   Ibid., p. 490.

41   Luther relied upon Augustine for his own theology. Luther's theological position on the self was definitely influenced by Augustine and his assertion that all is created by God.

"By this Trinity, supremely and equally and immutably good, were all things created. But they were not created supremely equal nor immutably good, and taken as a whole they are very good, because together they constitute a universe of admirable beauty."

Augustine, <u>Enchiridion</u> (London: SCM Press, 1955), p. 342. And again in Augustine:

"Every actual entity (natura) is therefore good: a greater good if it cannot be corrupted, a lesser good if it can be. Yet only the foolish and unknowing can deny that it is still good even when corrupted." Ibid., p. 340.

42   Jean Calvin, Institutes of the Christian Religion (Philadelphia: Westminster Press, 1960) I, p. 35.

43   Ibid., I, p. 35.

44   Ibid., I, p. 36.

45   Ibid.

46   Ibid., I. p. 37.

47   Ibid., I, p. 38.

❈ Chapter Four ❦

Loneliness is needy - it wants.
Solitude is fulfillment - it has. [1]
Sister Wendy

NARCISSISM AND DISTORTION

In the previous chapter narcissism was characterized as involving a loss of object relations, exhibitionism, infantilism, the development of the grandiose fantasy, and ultimately, as Stuart states, the loss of the self in self-hatred. Self-hatred expresses itself as immaturity and selfishness. Robert Salinger provides a good summary of the pathological characteristics a narcissist demonstrates:

> *Individuals with pathological narcissism are characterized clinically by their excessive interest in themselves, their lack of interest in other people, and the immature relationships they have with significant others who serve primarily as a mirror to reflect the overinvolvement with the self... They have low self-esteem, low self-confidence, feelings of emptiness or deadness, shyness, fears of rejection and a tendency to withdraw.*[2]

Salinger contends that these characteristics not only lead to a distorted perception of the self but also lead to religious distortion as well. I agree and state further that for the narcissist God becomes not an entity separate from the self to be obeyed and loved but simply one more entity to be manipulated. Luther writes that the self curved in upon itself is the sinful self that ".... seeks everything, including God, only for itself."[3] This describes the religious position of the narcissist today. Through this process both the self and God are demeaned.

Salinger adopts the concepts of Kohut for his discussion of narcissism in religion. These are: primary narcissism, the idealized parent imago or ego ideal, and the narcissistic self.

Primary narcissism plays a part in early religious experience, that is, one's conversion and subsequent experience of the relationship with God. The parallel between these two lies in one's early experience of God as similar to one's infant experience of the mother. In this instance the narcissist perceives that there is no separation between himself or herself and the mother. Salinger states:

> *Just as the primary narcissism of the infant flows out of the union of the infant with the mother, the bliss of the new convert flows out of a newfound union with God.[4]*

The infant must perceive that separation between himself or herself and the mother exists in order to mature. For the convert to mature in faith he or she must perceive that a fundamental difference exists between God and the self. In periods of deep prayer or in significant times of worship, an experience of one's early unity with God may be stirred, but a faith relationship with God must include a recognition that God is fundamentally different from the self.[5] The process just described involves growth in faith and trust in God and letting go of the notion that one must constantly experience a particular emotional state in order for God to be real.[6]

The idealized parent imago is the next concept of Kohut that Salinger explores. The concept involves the development by the child of an idealized parent who is capable of meeting all the child's needs. This parent is seen as a source of gratification, and therefore worthy of the child's love. The child becomes frustrated with the imperfection of the mother's ministrations and so creates an idealized parent who will not frustrate the child. This process takes place in response to the absence of a parent through work, mental and physical illness, and emotional withdrawal for whatever reason. Many of the characteristics of the idealized parent become internalized and form the ego ideal. The ego ideal incorporates moral standards, ideals, and values. Because self-esteem is measured through comparison with the lofty ego ideal, the person, as a result, generally suffers with low self-esteem.

The idealized parent imago, in narcissistic religious conversion, becomes projected upon God. This development is the most frequently identified process by psychoanalysts in their attack upon religion. Freud states:

> *Man's self-regard, seriously menaced, calls for consolation; life and the universe must be robbed of their terrors; moreover his curiosity, moved, it is true, by the strongest practical interest, demands an answer.[7]*

Freud asserts that this answer is sought in a human's striving for a father and longing for the gods. The function of the gods is threefold:

> *...they must exorcise the terrors of nature, they must reconcile men to the cruelty of Fate, particularly as it is shown in death, and they must compensate them for the sufferings and privations which a civilized life in common has imposed on them.[8]*

For Freud, the father god worshipped by Jews and Christian alike is nothing more than a cosmic projection of an early father-complex.

The attitude just stated remains prevalent among psychoanalysts and secular society today, in spite of attacks upon it by the clergy, laity, and intellectuals within religious faiths. The continued acceptance of Freud's work, <u>Totem and Taboo</u>, is evidence of this fact. In this work Freud alleges that the basis for social organization, moral restriction, and religion is all traceable to this story:

> *In the beginning, all the females were kept by the father. He was jealous and would drive his sons off as they became sexual, desiring to keep all the females for himself. Ultimately the expelled sons returned, killed their father and ate him. They appropriated all his females as well.*[9]

Freud writes that the remembrance and repetition of this story in ritual form is the fundamental event celebrated in religious faith.

Mircea Eliade calls Freud's <u>Totem and Taboo</u> a *"wild gothic novel"*. [10] He notes that Wilhelm Schmidt has written that the cannibalism allegedly present among pretotemic peoples was unheard of and that the patricide described by Freud in his book was a:

> *sheer impossibility, psychologically, sociologically, (and) ethically.*[11]

Freud's attack upon religion has more to do with social fashion than responsible scholarly work.

Nevertheless, the narcissistic projection of the idealized parent imago upon God has elements of this bad faith described by Freud. For the narcissist, God is not there to help a person deal with frustrations; rather, God is there to protect the narcissistic self from experiencing frustrations at all. Neither of these adaptations can be called true religious faith. Both are distortions and therefore serve merely as critiques of bad faith. These critiques provide the church with models of bad faith to avoid.

Scripture is an important measure for faith. Through scripture the convert is called to form a new ego ideal which involves being "...conformed to the image of (Jesus Christ)..." (Romans 8:29 RSV.) The person then realizes that internalizing and imitating Jesus Christ is the standard for true faith. As stated in Galatians 2:20a "...I have been crucified with Christ; it is no longer I who live, but Christ who lives in me..."

In contrast to the idealized parent imago, which is the result of a person's struggle toward love, perfection, and the avoidance of frustration, the narcissistic self is the aspect of the self which wants to be looked at and admired. The narcissistic self incorporates the concepts described in the previous chapter, namely, exhibitionism and the grandiose fantasy. These two attributes may lead a person, through religious conversion, "...to say, I must be pretty special to have been accepted by God, rather than, God is pretty special for having accepted me."[12] Jesus dealt with self-exaltation and personal ambition in his disciples (Matt. 20: 20-28; Mark 8:34-38, 10:35-44; Luke 22:24-30). Jesus did not criticize them for being ambitious "per se" but for attempting to advance themselves beyond the purposes of God. Jesus taught the disciples that they were to give up personal ambition in favor of being ambitious in their service of God and one another.

THE CONDITION OF SIN IN TILLICH

Tillich's understanding of sin as estrangement is very similar to the understanding of narcissism as isolation. Estrangement is marked by unbelief, "hubris", and concupiscence, and involves separation from God, the self, and others. Narcissistic isolation is characterized by the loss of the self and involves separation from others and the self through self-hatred. Both sin and narcissism participate in self-delusion and a grandiose fantasy about the extent of one's power. The comparison between sin and narcissism will be drawn more carefully later, but for now I will give a brief summary of Tillich's systematic theology.

Tillich understands his theological task as one of interpreting the Christian message to a new generation. In order to be comprehensible by a new generation it must address the crucial questions asked by that generation about existence. It, in order to be called Christian theology, must show how Jesus as the Christ, the revelation of New Being, is the answer to these questions.

He calls this method the method of correlation. Tillich explains that, like an apologetic,

> ..(this) method of correlation explains the contents of the Christian faith through existential questions and theological answers in mutual interdependence.[13]

Tillich pursues this task by assessing human existence and its distortions. He states that humans in existence are estranged from essential nature[14] and are not what they essentially are or ought to be.[15] The essential nature of humans is one of union with God, who is "being" itself and bestows being upon us. Our essential nature is one of true humanity marked by reconciliation and peace. But humans in existence do not participate in essential nature. Rather, humans know existence as estrangement and dehumanization. As Tillich states, existence "is the process in which man becomes a thing and ceases to be a person."[16] In becoming estranged and dehumanized a person becomes threatened with self-destruction. This threat fills a person with meaninglessness and anxiety. The human condition is marked by a fall from essence to existence. The myth of Adam and Eve, in Genesis chapters 1-3, is pointed to by Tillich and called by him a symbolic description of the transition from essence to existence. The Fall, as such, does not constitute a break but an imperfect fulfillment of the historical process. Two factors make for the possibility of the Fall: God's statement of prohibition and the human condition of anxiety. The myth of the Fall is valuable in that it describes the human existential predicament of self-estrangement.[17]

The fall from essence to existence takes place by a person's actualizing finite freedom. Finite freedom is not complete freedom but anxious freedom. God alone has complete freedom. Human freedom is limited by one's finitude or mortality. [18]

Finite freedom is possessed by a person in "dreaming innocence" or the original state of union with God—the ground of all being. Both of the words <u>dreaming</u> and <u>innocence</u> describe a point which comes before actual existence. "Dreaming innocence" contains potentiality, but not actuality. It is the state preceding actuality, existence, and history, but it is not a state of perfection. In the words of Tillich, "Only the conscious union of existence and essence is perfection, as God is perfect because he transcends essence and existence."[19]

Human existence, limited by finiteness, is filled with anxiety as the possibility for nonbeing is always present from the position of anxiety and separation.

The shock of nonbeing causes one to be aware of the fact that existence contains the potential for radical negation. Nonbeing is the dialectical opposite of being. One's ability to perceive one's being and nonbeing is due to the fact that one participates in each. It involves separation from being and is marked by the presence of anxiety. Questions to ask are: "How can I continue to be?", and, "Where is the basis for the courage to be?" Tillich's answer is in the doctrine of God in his <u>Systematic Theology</u>, Vol. I. He states that God is the ground of all being and the power of being in everything. Only through the "power of being-itself is the creature able to resist nonbeing."[20] The power of being-itself is the power of infinite love that desires reunion with that which has become estranged.

Humans within the existential situation have another urgent question, though. Aware of his or her estrangement from essence and participation in contradiction, a human asks about salvation, or the possibility of new being. The structure of being has been disrupted by finitude and is characterized by polarities. It is now basically a subject-object structure with the self-world structure broken into three elements, indicated by the following polarities: individualization and participation; dynamics and form; and freedom and destiny. The human self has potentialities (dynamis) which must take some form. The question now is: How can these potentialities take form without becoming chaotic on the one hand or rigid on the other? In other words, how many persons can realize their freedom without defying their destiny, and in doing so lose the direction and meaning of their lives?

In order to protect his or her individuality a person attempts to resolve the previously stated polarities in favor of individuality, potentiality, and freedom. But a person's attempt at self-salvation will ultimately fail, for he or she is able to act only within this condition of estrangement and all the limitations present within the condition of estrangement and all the limitations present within this condition. In his <u>Systematic Theology</u>, Vol. II, Tillich presents that the answer to this question is Jesus as the Christ - Jesus through whom the power of New Being is manifested. Through receiving Jesus as the Christ, the New Being, one discovers himself or herself accepted and empowered to function as a new being also.[21]

TILLICH AND THE COMPARISON BETWEEN PSYCHOANALYTIC THEORY AND THE CONDITION OF SIN

In Tillich, turning from God is an expression of both freedom and guilt; freedom, in that one is capable of making the choice to turn away from that to which he or she belongs, and guilt, in that one's choices incur responsibility. To sin is not simply to violate moral codes, but also to separate oneself from God, the self, and others. It involves choosing the self over God and results in one's loss of a true and united self.[22] The three marks of estrangement, noted above, are unbelief, "hubris", and concupiscence.

Unbelief is the act of turning away from God in knowledge, will, and emotion. It is the separation of the human will from God's will, characterized by Tillich as not simply denying Christian dogma about God, Jesus as the Christ, Creation, etc., but turning away from that to which one belongs. Tillich uses Augustine to describe this turn as love turned from God to the self. The act of turning, in terms of love, involves not only turning from God but also turning from proper to distorted love of self and the world. Love of self and world is proper if one loves the self and the world as finite manifestations of the infinite reality—God. If one loves finite reality, manifested in the self and the world, without recognizing one's origin in an infinite God, distortion takes place. This involves distortion in both love and faith.[23] Distorted faith is faith that invests finite reality with infinite value. Unbelief is estrangement in terms of love and faith.

Narcissism involves turning away from something as well. In the myth of Narcissus, Narcissus turned away from the love offered to him by several nymphs only later to fall tragically in love with his own reflection. He cut himself off from others, and the love offered by them to him, in favor of indulging in the self-consuming love, from which he died. Narcissism is characterized by the psychoanalysts I reviewed as involving the loss of object love. Kohut speaks of how the narcissist demonstrates an exhibitionist tendency placing emphasis upon the pleasure of the narcissist in the role of performer rather than the other as observer. The potential role of the other, in terms of providing love and support, is neglected by the narcissist in favor of isolated, self-consuming, and ultimately self-destructive "love." This kind of love is negative narcissism for Kohut, Kernberg, and Grunberger. It is self-hatred or an act of the not-self for Stuart.

The second mark of estrangement for Tillich is "hubris" or self-elevation. It involves self-elevation to the realm of the divine. Through estrangement, humans find themselves outside of the divine center to which their own centers belong. Humans attempt to fill this void, the loss of a center, with themselves. "Hubris" has been called the "spiritual sin", for it is sin in its total form. Unbelief is the turning away from that to which one belongs and "hubris", turning toward the self as the center of one's self and one's world, is the consequence. The result of "hubris" is that humans refuse to acknowledge their finitude. They confuse their limited goodness with absolute goodness. "Hubris" is possible because of the greatness of humans within creation. The temptation for humans because of their greatness is to make the self the center of oneself and one's world. This was the flaw, time and again, of Greek heroes in the Greek tragedies.[24]

Because of one's self-perceived greatness within the scheme of creation, a person is unwilling to acknowledge the fact of one's finitude, weakness, errors, insecurity, loneliness, and anxiety. These are attributes of the narcissist also. They are found in Kernberg as well as in Kohut, Grunberger, and Stuart, but to these attributes Kernberg adds emptiness, restlessness, and boredom. Kohut states that dealing with one's finitude is important for transcending negative narcissism. All of these attributes listed by Tillich are found in the work of Stuart and the psychoanalysts reviewed here, indicating the presence of similar distortions in sin and narcissism.

The third mark of estrangement found in sin is concupiscence. In the distorted self, the desire for reunion with that from which one is separated involves a desire to control and possess. The desire to control and possess results in an evil use of power. It creates the potential for the elevation of the self beyond particularity and the megalomaniacal misuse of power. In the state of concupiscence a person attempts to draw the whole of reality into the self. Tillich uses Emperor Nero as an illustration of the destructive potential of concupiscence, for, when Nero realized that he could not control and possess Rome, he chose to burn it instead. He could not draw the whole of it into himself so he chose to destroy it.[25]

Tillich refers to concupiscence as having sexual implications. He states that sexual concupiscence involves the desire to want our pleasure through another, but not to want the other person for himself or herself. Pleasure is taken from another person without desiring that person in his or her entirety. Tillich defines concupiscence as distorted libido.[26]

The extension of the self beyond one's particularity is especially characteristic of the narcissist. Loss of object relations takes place for the narcissist because of the loss of the self and with it awareness of one's parameters. The narcissist views others as extensions of the self and therefore they lose their "otherness." As extensions of the self they become subject to the desires and whims of the self and lose all rights as separate individuals.

In this chapter I have discussed the theology of Paul Tillich and demonstrated how discussion of sin as estrangement relates to psychoanalytic work in the area of narcissism. A definite link exists between Tillich's discussion of estrangement as unbelief, "hubris", and concupiscence and psychoanalytically purported characteristics of narcissism. The importance of recognizing this link is that the church can see how it participates in narcissistic distortion. By understanding narcissism as sin, self-loss and self-hatred, the Christian disciple may begin to reassess how he or she speaks of sin and salvation in the modern era. The Christian disciple must reexamine his or her commitment to the message of Jesus Christ and how it speaks about the love of God. God's love is not sentimental and hollow, but forgiving and suffering. God's justice calls all into accountability and bestows upon us dignity and freedom, as well as personal responsibility and the requirement for complete commitment to God. God's mercy comes out of God's suffering with the people and cannot be trivialized by us through our efforts to manipulate it. As Salinger states:

> *To deal effectively with the problem of narcissism, the church must develop an evangelistic message which at the same time welcomes all people and caters to none.*[27]

The present church has abandoned its own historical writings on the self and has adopted the modern secular doctrine of pseudo-self-awareness instead. Paul Vitz discusses this development but attributes it to the liberal church alone. He states that psychology has become a rival religion to Christianity in America. Psychology espouses "selfism" in contrast to the selflessness maintained in Christian doctrine.[28] But Shirley Guthrie, Jr., finds the presence of selfishness within all Christian churches, and it has more to do with our distortion of God and ourselves than with an outright attack by proponents of psychology. The church distorts God through talking about what God will do <u>for</u> you and how little it requires <u>of</u> you. The church distorts the classic position of Christianity concerning the self represented here by Luther and Calvin. It has adopted the Transactional Analysis assurance that "I'm O.K.—You're O.K.," and has not genuinely talked about what it has cost God to re-establish us as redeemed from sin and separation. By participating in these secular assumptions, the church is not telling the truth about God or the self.[29]

The church, by not taking the effect of narcissism upon it seriously, is not only distorting the truth about God and the self but is also trivializing the importance of God, the self, and religious faith. Psychoanalytic work in the area of narcissism reveals crucial characteristics present with selves disrupted by narcissism and may assist the church in discovering how it exemplifies and encourages narcissistic faith. The church has ignored the impact of narcissism upon it. It has made it difficult for people genuinely to know and love God; know and love themselves as children of God; know and love others as themselves.

Recapturing the awareness that who God is and what God has done for us through Jesus as the Christ is costly and is vital for the Christian. Discipleship requires that we know ourselves as selves, loved and created good by God; possessing dignity and purpose through God's mercy.

The question still remains for us: Is it possible to create a "realistic self-concept" (in the words of the psychoanalysts) without first dealing with guilt, both personal and social? The answer to this question is "no." Guilt is a problem dealt with in Christian theology by the doctrine of salvation. In the next chapter we will examine Tillich's doctrinal development of salvation and compare it to Kohut's thought on the transformation of narcissism.

ENDNOTES - CHAPTER 4

1   Sister Wendy, <u>Conversation with Bill Moyer</u>, Copyright 1997, WGBH Educational Foundation.

2   Robert J. Salinger, "Narcissism and Conversion: Implications for Evangelism," <u>CAPS Bulletin</u>, V:2 (1979),

3   Martin Luther, <u>Lectures on Romans</u>, (Philadelphia: Westminster Press, 1961), p. 159.

4   Salinger, p. 31.

5   Abraham Heschel supports this notion in his statement that:

Nowhere in the Bible is man characterized as merciful, gracious, slow to anger, abundant in love and truth, keeping love to the thousandth generation...

God's unconditional concern for justice is not anthropomorphism. Rather, man's concern for justice is theomorphism.

Abraham J. Heschel, <u>The Prophets</u> (San Francisco, Harper & Row, 1963) II, 51-52.

6   Salinger, p. 31.

7   Sigmund Freud, <u>The Future of an Illusion</u> (Garden City; Doubleday, 1927), p. 22.

8   Ibid.

9   Sigmund Freud, <u>Totem and Taboo</u> (New York: Norton, 1950), pp. 1-17.

10   Mircea Eliade, <u>Occultism, Witchcraft, and Cultural Fashions</u> (Chicago: University of Chicago Press, 1976), p. 4.

11   Ibid.

12   Salinger, p. 33.

13   Paul Tillich, <u>Systematic Theology</u> (Chicago: University of Chicago:University of Chicago Press, 1967), I, 60.

14   Ibid., II, 25.

15   Ibid., II, 45.

16   Ibid., II, 25.

17   Ibid., II, 24 ff.

18   Ibid., II, 31-32.

19   Ibid., II, 34.

20   Ibid., I, 261.

21   Ibid., II, 78 ff.

22   Ibid., II, 29 ff.

23   Ibid., II, 47-49.

24   Ibid., II, 49-51.

25   Ibid., II, 52-53.

26   Ibid., II, 51-55.

27   Salinger, p. 34.

28   Paul Vitz, <u>Psychology as Religion</u> (Grand Rapids, Eerdmans, 1977).

29   Shirley C. Guthrie, Jr., "The Narcissism of American Piety: The Disease and the Cure," <u>Journal of Pastoral Care</u>, XXXI (December 1977) 221-226.

❖ Chapter Five ❖

"Christt, you know I love you!
Did you see me wave?
I believe in you and God,
so tell me that I'm saved!"[1]
From the movie,
"Jesus Christ Superstar"

While he was saying this, a
woman in the crowd raised her
voice and said to him, "Blessed is
the womb that bore you and the
breasts that nursed you!" But he
said, "Blessed rather are those
who hear the word of God and
obey it!"[2]
Luke 11: 27-28

KOHUT

Heinz Kohut notes four characteristics of the personality which are necessary for the transformation of the narcissistic personality disorder. They are "his ability to be empathetic, his capacity to contemplate impermanence, his sense of humor, his wisdom."[3]

Kohut defines empathy as "the mode by which one gathers psychological data about other people and, when they say what they think or feel, imagines their inner experience even though it is not open to direct observation."[4] He believes that training in empathy is an important part of psychoanalytic training and helps loosen the narcissistic perspective a person has of his or her surroundings. A person's increased ability to recognize another person as separate from the self is vital if one is to practice empathy. This ability is a sign that a person is moving beyond the narcissistic preoccupation with the isolated self.

The recognition of one's finiteness is vital for the transformation of the narcissist. Kohut asserts that it is vital for the narcissist to face finitude for:

> *...without these efforts, a valid conception of time, of limits, and of the impermanence of the object cathexes (the concentration of psychic energy on some particular person, thing, idea, or aspect of the self) could not be achieved.*[5]

Acceptance of the impermanence of the self and others is an important step toward releasing the self from narcissistic absorption.

Kohut asserts that humor is a "uniquely human acquisition... which enables one to overcome the fear of death."[6] Overcoming the fear of death through humor takes place as one is able to joke about one's impending death and thus place oneself "upon a higher plane."[7] Kohut quotes a joke used by Freud to illustrate this process:

> *...a criminal who was being led out to the gallows on Monday remarked: "Well, the week's beginning nicely."*[8]

The criminal's use of humor was both liberating and satisfactory, for it enabled the criminal to overcome the fear of impending death. Humor allows a person to transform the demands of the narcissistic self by enabling him or her to face finiteness.

Kohut's final characteristic which enables the transformation of narcissism is wisdom. This characteristic enables one to accept the limitations of his or her physical, intellectual, and emotional abilities. "Wisdom involves forming a stable attitude...toward life and the world..."[9] This attitude of the personality involves the integration of humor, finitude, and a system of values into a whole. This is a cognitive process which involves the mind, but this wisdom is more than knowledge. It is not an isolated intellectual achievement, but the "victorious outcome of the lifework of the total personality..."[10] It goes beyond cognitive awareness yet incorporates it. It involves maturity through the acceptance of finitude and usually takes place during the later years of one's life.

TILLICH

What Kohut calls negative narcissism Paul Tillich calls evidence of the condition of sin. The solution to the condition of sin for Tillich is in salvation offered to us through Jesus Christ.

The condition of sin is characterized by three marks of estrangement — unbelief, "hubris" and concupiscence. These marks of estrangement involve turning away from God in both emotion and intellect, resulting in the elevation of the self to the realm of the divine. A common symptom is the misuse of one's power through the manipulation of one's world, or the overwhelming of others and the desire to draw the whole of reality into the self.[11] The atonement of condition of sin is one of reunion with that to which one belongs. Salvation is a reunion of the separated which is accomplished through Jesus as the Christ, who expresses symbolically the subjection of existence and the victory of essence. It is "healing" in that it "means reuniting that which is estranged, giving a center to that which is split, overcoming the split between God and man, man and his world, man and himself."[12]

Out of the above interpretation of salvation, the concept of New Being has come about. Salvation means that the world is made new; non-being has been replaced by being. Jesus as the Christ is the manifestation of New Being. He is the revelation of the healing power of New Being. He reveals that God is the power of being in people, things, and the world. Reunion with God takes place through one's acceptance of Jesus as the Christ, as New Being. Jesus as the Savior heals the separation of humans from each other and from themselves through reunion with the ground of being or God. Jesus as the Christ reveals the saving power of New Being.[13]

Jesus as the Christ manifests the reconciling act of God to humans but is not reconciliation in and of himself. Reconciliation is the outcome of atonement and the "atoning processes are created by God and God alone."[14] The guilt and punishment which stand between humans and Godself are reconciled by the mediation of the New Being in Christ, but God is not dependent upon the Christ. Rather, God chooses to reveal God's reconciling act toward humans through the

Christ, but God may do so in another fashion. This is the first of Tillich's principles of atonement.

The second is that in God there is no conflict between God's reconciling love and God's justice. God's justice is not punishment of the sinner, but God allowing the self-destructive consequences of estrangement to take their course. God cannot remove these consequences because they are a part of the structure of being in which God participates. To interrupt the structure of being is not love. Love is not "resisting and breaking what is against love."[15] Justice "is the structural form of love without which it would be sheer sentimentality."[16]

The third principle of atonement is that God's removal of our guilt is "not an act of overlooking the reality and depth of existential estrangement."[17] Divine and human forgiveness cannot be compared, for the human who forgives another human is guilty as well. Rather, God represents the order of being and violation of this is not an insignificant matter. Forgiveness cannot be private because of the magnitude of this break throughout the human condition.

The fourth principle of atonement is that God participates in existential estrangement and its destructive consequences. These consequences cannot be ignored, for they are implied in God's justice.

The fifth principle of atonement in the theology of Tillich is that "in the cross of the Christ the divine participation in existential estrangement becomes manifest."[18] This event is a manifestation through which God's work of salvation becomes actualized. It is a central manifestation in that, through it, God participates in the suffering of the world. Through the specter of the cross the guilty one sees God's act of atonement in and through the cross. God takes the consequences of atonement upon Godself.

The sixth principle of atonement is that through

participation in the New Being a person is participating in God's atoning act. The person takes part in the suffering of God in the Christ. This suffering involves participating in God's transforming action. God transforms a being and through participating in God's suffering, transformation from non-being to being becomes possible. Engaging in the divine participation requires that we accept God's saving action and are therein transformed.

Tillich discusses salvation as having a "threefold character...: participation, acceptance, transformation. (In classical terminology: regeneration, justification, sanctification.)"[19] The first trait, salvation by participation in the New Being (regeneration), involves participation in Jesus as the Christ, who is the manifestation of New Being. "The power of the New Being must lay hold of him who is still in bondage to the old being."[20] A person must be grasped and drawn into relation with the New Being, producing what the Apostle Paul called being in Christ. The characteristics of New Being are the opposite of the characteristics of estrangement. Instead of unbelief there is faith; instead of "hubris" there is surrender; instead of concupiscence there is love. A person is reborn through participation in New Being.[21]

The second trait involves salvation as acceptance of the New Being, or justification. This step presupposes faith—faith that is the "work of the divine Spirit, the power which creates the New Being in the Christ, in individuals, in the church."[22] Justification is the element of "in spite of" in salvation. God accepts the estranged "in spite of" his or her estrangement, drawing the estranged into unity with God. God, through the act of justification (literally "making just") restores a person's essentiality, from which he or she is estranged. This is an act which is of God and is not dependent upon humans. God accepts that which is unacceptable. This enables a person to look away from his or her "state of estrangement and self-destruction to the justifying act of God."[23] It is the only way in which a person can transcend his or her anxiety, guilt, and despair.

The third trait of salvation is sanctification, which is salvation as transformation by the New Being. Regeneration and justification both describe the reunion of what is estranged. They both involve the divine acceptance of the unacceptable. Sanctification is different from regeneration and justification in that it involves, through the power of New Being, the transformation of "personality and community, inside and outside the church."[25] The sanctifying work of the Spirit, actualized in the New Being, takes place in the individual Christian as well as in the church. Sanctification belongs to the categories found in Tillich's third volume of his Systematic Theology.

KOHUT AND TILLICH IN DIALOGUE

Kohut describes the transformation of narcissism as taking place through the development of the capacity to be empathetic and to contemplate one's impermanence, as well as develop a sense of humor and acquire wisdom. In Tillich transformation of a person from the condition of sin is accomplished through turning away from estrangement to the revelation of Jesus as the Christ.

Tillich deals with the problem of guilt by acknowledging that this is a serious, self-destructive element in human existence. Guilt can only be forgiven and transformed by God, who accepts the unacceptable and alone is able to justify and restore estranged humanity.

Kohut deals with guilt as a duality that is indeed serious. His solutions to negative narcissism sound a great deal like what Tillich calls "self-salvation," or the effort of a person to restore one's unity by oneself. Kohut views humanity from the perspective that it does indeed participate in distortion, but it is a distortion of the self brought about by inadequate parenting. Separation from God is not a problem in Kohut's research of narcissism. But, as I established in Chapter Four, there is a great deal of similarity between the characteristics of negative narcissism in Kohut and the condition of sin in Tillich. For this reason it can be asserted that narcissism may be dealt with as a condition of sin and that the transforming suggestions of Tillich on the condition of sin can be applied to the problem of negative narcissism in the individual and in the church.

The isolation of the narcissistic and estranged person is overcome through reunion with God. The grandiose self bound in narcissism and in "hubris" and concupiscence, "three elements in the condition of sin," may be healed through an encounter with the New Being, which is Jesus as the Christ. The Christ reveals this kind of self-elevation as distortion, coming from non-being and separation from the ground of being. The creation of a grandiose notion of the self, as well as the self-elevation found in sin, is a response to one's awareness of separation and is an attempt to protect the self from anxiety. These attempts to protect the self from anxiety fail, for they do not deal with the problem of genuine guilt.

Self-hatred is a powerful element found in negative narcissism and the condition of sin. One cannot begin to love the self by simply deciding that it is important to do so. Tillich takes care of this problem by stating that acceptance and love of the self are possible because God loves, accepts and transforms us. They are possible because of God's action to restore us and God's willingness to suffer the consequences with us, as revealed in the cross. The transformation of self-hatred into self-love is possible because of God's participation with humanity from the source of being.

It has been asserted that both narcissism and distortion are brought about through participation in the condition of sin, dealt with through the revelation of New Being manifested in Jesus as the Christ. No form of distortion and separation is outside of God's restoring action. All forms of distortion can be overcome and healed through God's effort at restoring that which is separated: the self, others, and, in Tillichean theology, from God as the ground of being.

Through accepting Jesus as the Christ we become a participant in New Creation. As Tillich states in his sermon, "The New Being,"

> *Christianity is the message of the New Creation, the New Being, the New Reality...For the Christ, the Messiah, the selected and anointed one is He who brings the new state of things.*[26]

God takes the task upon Godself because, as the first letter of John states, "God is love..." (4:16). In Tillich's sermon, "The Power of Love," he makes it clear that, as in First John, to live in God is to live in love. As Tillich states, "God and love are not two realities; they are one." God is love and therefore takes the destructive old order upon Godself, creating a new order marked by reunion of that which is separated.

In this book it has been demonstrated that similarities between narcissism and Tillich's theological interpretation of the condition of sin exist. The relationship between the two are in the characteristics that they share, namely: (1) turning away from others and toward the self; (2) grandiosity or self-elevation; (3) isolation; (4) a misuse of one's power to draw the whole of reality into the self or the manipulation of others for one's own gain; (5) self-hatred and anxiety;

(6) the loss of the self and the other through self-absorption and self-hatred.

Christian Churches need to deal with the distortion of narcissism and sin, not by adopting the attributes of narcissism, but by helping people recognize and restore a healthy relationship with God.

Any healthy relationship with God must begin with our repentance turning our faces away from gazing upon ourselves but rather gazing upon the cross of Christ.

> *Then Jesus said to his disciple, 'If anyone wants to be a follower of mine, let him renounce himself and take up his cross and follow me. Anyone who wants to save his life will lose it; but anyone who loses his life for my sake will find it.'*

Matthew 16: 24-25

> *Then speaking to all, he said, 'If anyone wants to be a follower of mine, let him renounce himself and take up his cross every day and follow me. Anyone who wants to save his life will lose it; but anyone who loses his life for my sake, will save it.*

Luke 9: 23-24

This glorious opportunity is ours to respond to God's grace. God's gift is available to each of us, and now is the day of salvation.

To God be the Glory, the Majesty, and the Honor, forever and ever.

Amen

ENDNOTES - CHAPTER FIVE

1   The movie, "Jesus Christ Superstar," Norman Jewison-Robert Stigwood Production, 1973.

2   Ibid

3   Heinz Kohut, <u>The Search for the Self</u> (New York: International University Press, 1978), p. 446.

4   Ibid., p. 450.

5   Ibid., p. 454.

6   Ibid., p. 456.

7   Ibid.

8   Ibid.

9   Ibid., p. 458.

10   Ibid., p. 459.

11   Paul Tillich, <u>Systematic Theology</u> (Chicago: University of Chicago Press, 1967), II, 44ff.

12   Ibid., II, p. 166.

13   Ibid., II, p. 168ff.

14   Ibid., II, p.173

15   Ibid., II, p. 174.

16   Ibid.

17   Ibid.

18   Ibid.

19   Ibid., II, p. 175.

20   Ibid.

21   Ibid., II, p. 177.

22   Ibid., II, p. 178.

23   Ibid.

24   Ibid., II, p. 180.

25   Paul Tillich, <u>The New Being</u> (New York: Charles Scribner's Sons, 1955), p.15.

❋❴ Bibliography ❵❋

BOOKS

Augustine. <u>Enchiridon: On Faith, Hope, and Love</u>, ed. Albert C. Outler. (Library of Christian Classics, 7) London: S.C.M. Press, 1955.

Baldwin, James. <u>Giovanni's Room</u>. New York: Dial Press, 1956.

Bonhoeffer, Dietrich. <u>The Cost of Discipleship</u>. New York: Simon and Schuster, 1959.

Bugliosi, Vincent. <u>Outrage: The Five Reasons Why O. J. Simpson Got Away with Murder</u>. New York, London: W.W. Norton and Company, 1996.

Calvin, Jean. <u>Institutes of the Christian Religion</u>, ed. John T. McNeill. 2 vols. (Library of Christian Classics, 20-21) Philadelphia: Westminster Press, 1960.

Eliade, Mircea. <u>Occultism, Witchcraft, and Cultural Fashions</u>, Chicago: University of Chicago Press, 1976.

Flugel, J.C. <u>Man, Morals and Society</u>. New York: International University Press, 1945.

Freud, Sigmund:

<u>Collected Papers</u>, ed. Ernest Jones. 20 vols. New York: Basic Books, 1959.

<u>Totem and Taboo</u>, tr. James Strachey. New York: Norton, 1950.

<u>The Future of an Illusion</u>, tr. W. D. Robson-Scott, rev. and newly ed. by James Strachey. Garden City, New York: Doubleday, 1927.

Graves, Robert. <u>The Greek Myths, Book III</u>. Quoted by Shirley Sugarman. <u>Sin and Madness</u>. Philadelphia: Westminster Press, 1979.

Grunberger, Béla. <u>Narcissism and Psychoanalytic Essays</u>. New York:International University Press, 1971.

Hamilton, Edith. <u>Mythology</u>. Boston: Little, Brown and Company, 1942.

Heschel, Abraham. <u>The Prophets</u>, 2 vols. San Francisco: Harper & Row, 1963.

Horder, William E. <u>A Layman's Guide to Protestant Theology</u>. New York: Collier McMillan Publishers, London, Eighth Printing, 1974.

Jacoby, Russell. <u>Social Amnesia: A Critique of Conformist Psychologyfrom Adler to Laing</u>. Boston: Beacon Press, 1975.

Kernberg, Otto. <u>Borderline Conditions and Pathological Narcissism</u>. New York: Anderson, 1975.

Kohut, Heinz:
     <u>The Analysis of the Self: A Systematic Approach to thePsychoanalytic Treatment of Narcissistic Personality Disorders</u>. New York: International University Press, 1971.

     <u>The Search for the Self: Selected Writings</u>, ed. and introduction by Paul H. Ornstein. New York: International University Press, 1978.

Luther, Martin:

>Selections from his Writings, ed. John Dillenberger. Garden City: Doubleday, 1961.

>Lectures on Romans. (Library of Christian Classics, XV) ed. Wilhelm Pauck. Philadelphia: Westminster Press, 1961.

Outler, Albert. John Wesley. New York: Oxford University Press, 1964.

Petrocelli, David. Triumph of Justice. New York: Crown Publishers, 1998.

Sennett, Richard. The Fall of Public Man. New York: Knopf, 1977.

Stuart, Grace. Narcissus: A Psychological Study of Self-Love. London: Allen & Irwin, 1956.

Sugarman, Shirley. Sin and Madness: Studies in Narcissism. Philadelphia: Westminster Press, 1979.

Tillich, Paul:

>Systematic Theology. 3 vols. in one. Chicago: University of Chicago Press, 1967.

>The New Being. New York: Charles Scribner's Sons, 1955.

>The Shaking of the Foundations. New York: Charles Scribner's Sons, 1948.

Vitz, Paul. Psychology as Religion: The Cult of Self-Worship. Grand Rapids: Eerdman, 1977.

Bibliography

Zimmerli, Walter. <u>Old Testament Theology in Outline</u>, tr. David E. Green. Atlanta: John Knox Press, 1978.

ARTICLES

Guthrie, Shirley C., Jr. "The Narcissism of American Piety: The Disease and the Cure." <u>Journal of Pastoral Care</u>. XXXI (December 1977), 222.

Marin, Peter. "The New Narcissism." <u>Harper's</u>, CCLI (October 1975), 56.

Rechin, Bill and Wilder, Don. Cartoon: <u>Crook</u>. North American Syndicate, Inc., 1992.

Salinger, Robert J. "Narcissism and Conversion: Implications for Evangelism." <u>CAPS Bulletin</u> V:2 (1979).

Satow, Roberta. "Pop Narcissism." <u>Psychology Today</u>, XIII (October 1979).

Timnick, Lois. Quote from eulogy for Dr. Heinz Kohut. Written by Lois Timnick, staff writer, Los Angeles Times 1981.

Wolfe, Thomas. "The 'Me' Decade and the Third Great Awakening." <u>New York</u>, XXIII (August 1976), 26-40.

FILMS, TELEVISION, INTERNET

<u>All About Eve,</u> Released by 20th Century Fox. Directed by Joseph L. Mankiecwicz, 1950.

<u>Britannica Home Page</u>, Encyclopaedia Britannica, Inc. 1996.

"Jesus Christ Superstar", Norman Jewison. Robert Stigwood Production, 1973.

"Perfect", Produced and directed by James Bridges, 1985.

"Sister Wendy", Conversation with Bill Moyer, WGBH Educational Foundation, 1997.

RECOMMENDATIONS FOR FURTHER READING

Heschel, Abraham Joshua. Man Is Not Alone: a Philosophy of Religion. New York: Farrar, Straus, and Giroux, Inc. Paperback 1976.

Norris, Kathleen. The Cloister Walk. New York: Riverhead Books 1996.

Pascal, Blaise. The Thoughts of Blaise Pascal. Westport, Connecticut: Greenwood Publishing Group 1978.

Lasch, Christopher. The Culture of Narcissism: American Life in an Ageof Diminishing Expectations. New York: Warner Books, 1979.

❈ Biography ❊

     During a Multiple Sclerosis induced coma, Dr. Susan Lemly experienced an awakening, seemingly for the first time, to God's profound love. This profound love has not been adequately expressed to God's children by our contemporary Christian churches. Dr. Lemly considers that our contemporary churches have become deeply saturated in our contemporary culture. This narcissistic culture holds the belief that says, *me first, now and always!* This is antithetical to the preaching of Jesus Christ and the model of discipleship to God that He displayed. An example of this can be found in Paul's letter to the Philippians where he writes,

Who, though he was in the form of God, did not count equality with God a thing to be grasped, but emptied himself, taking the form of a servant, being born in the likeness of men. And being found in human form he humbled himself and became obedient unto death, even death on a cross.

Philippians 2: 6 – 8

Dr. Lemly graduated with a Bachelors of Arts, in 1976 from the University of Redlands, with a major in Religion and a minor in Psychology. After this she attended the School of Theology at Claremont, graduating in 1981 with a Masters of Divinity and a Doctor of Ministry. She was an Associate Pastor at the First United Methodist Church in San Diego from 1981 to 1983. In the summer of 1983 Dr. Lemly moved to Indianapolis, IN, to begin work on her Clinical Pastoral Education at Methodist Hospital with hopes of working as a hospital Chaplain. In late summer of that year, the effects of Multiple Sclerosis had progressed to a point that required full-time nursing care. Her parents, Harry and Eleanor Lemly, provided for her daily care for many years until their death, her mother being the last to die on July 24, 1998. She currently resides in a nursing care facility in Orange County, CA.

Christian Discipleship and ME is Dr. Lemly's first book.

For additional copies of, *Christian Discipleship and ME,* please send a check for $12.95 plus $3.95 for shipping and handling for each book. Make the check out to, Total Support Group, and send book order to:

Total Support Group
P. O. Box 6103
Oceanside, CA 92052-6103